ABSEN

Edited by Ruth Watts Davies

**Based on The Industrial Society course
'Absenteeism – a practical workshop'
devised by Gill Cobau and Sonia Pearson**

The Industrial Society

First published 1989 by
The Industrial Society
Robert Hyde House
48 Bryanston Square
London W1H 7LN
Telephone: 01-831 8388

© The Industrial Society, 1989

ISBN 0 85290 442 8

British Library Cataloguing in Publication Data
Watts-Davies, Ruth
   Absenteeism.—5th ed—(Notes for Managers)
   I. Title
   1. Personnel, Absenteeism. Management aspects
   658.3'14

Typeset by Ace Filmsetting Ltd, Frome, Somerset
Printed and bound in Great Britain by Belmont Press, Northampton

CONTENTS

FOREWORD

Whatever the discipline or level of management, the responsibilities of a manager are many and various. It is their job to produce results with essentially just two resources—people and time.

To maximise the potential of both, most managers need some reminders and basic guidelines to help them.

The Notes for Managers series provides succinct yet comprehensive coverage of key management issues and skills. The short time it takes to read each title will pay dividends in terms of utilising one of those key resources—people.

ALISTAIR GRAHAM
Director, The Industrial Society

1

INTRODUCTION

In a climate of increasing need for economic efficiency, absence and absenteeism from work is now the focus of considerable attention. Managers need to acquire the skills to understand what kind of absence is occurring within their organisations and to devise effective methods for getting the employees back to work at the earliest date, relevant to the circumstances.

Before a company can decide if it has an absence problem it has to have information. This enables it to make judgments about the size of the problem and to decide what action should be taken to improve the situation. This book therefore aims to:

- investigate the costs of absenteeism to the organisation
- examine the methods of monitoring absenteeism and their costs
- identify the causes of absenteeism
- identify practical ways of reducing the level of absenteeism
- consider the legal and practical framework.

2

MEASURING THE COST
OF ABSENTEEISM

Before it is possible to consider or implement any policy to control absenteeism, it is necessary to consider:

● what form does it take?
● how many employees are involved?
● how much does it cost?

What form does it take?

When looking at absence, holidays are normally ignored as these are authorised. There are, however, a number of other forms that absence takes:

● sickness—certified; self-certified; suspension on medical grounds
● statutory time off
● strikes/industrial action
● special leave absence—sabbaticals
● personal/domestic
● lateness
● unauthorised/casual leave.

Absence must be measured in both terms of duration (severity) and episodes (frequency). One measure alone can be misleading, as a single calculation cannot describe the situation adequately. Most firms produce some sort of lost time rate and this method of calculation is preferred by accountants, as time can be easily costed. Frequency rates, however, are more valuable references in planning absence controls.

The three main methods of calculation normally used are as follows.

1 *Lost time rate*

$$\frac{\text{No. of days lost through absence}}{\text{Average number of employees} \times \text{working days}} \times 100$$

2 *Number of employees affected*

$$\frac{\text{No. of employees with one or more absence spells}}{\text{Average number of employees over the period}} \times 100$$

3 *Average length of absence*

$$\frac{\text{Total days lost in period of absence}}{\text{Number of spells of absence}}$$

The 'average number of employees' is taken as the average number employed over the period for which the absenteeism statistic is being calculated.

The 'average number of working days' is worked out by calculating the number of possible working days over the period for which the absenteeism statistic is being calculated.

Example:

The national absence rate of 5.05% per annum found in The Industrial Society survey *Absence rates and control policies* (1987) was calculated according to the following formula.

$$\frac{\text{Total no. of days lost through absence during year} \times 100}{\text{No. of employees} \times 230 \text{ working days}}$$

The resulting figure is the absence rate in percentage terms. The figure of 230 working days was arrived at by the following calculation:

52 weeks × 5 working days	260 days
Less 8 statutory days	− 8 days
	252 days
Less 22 days holiday	− 22 days
	230 days

How much does it cost?

Once the levels of absenteeism have been calculated it is possible to start considering the costs to the company. These come from a number of different sources, some of which are obvious. For example:

- the cost of sick pay schemes
- the costs of providing temporary cover
- increased overtime costs
- loss of production.

There are, however, hidden costs which, if taken into account, amount to a considerable expense. These can include:

- increased pressure on administrative time as a result of changing rotas or administering sick pay
- increased pressure on supervisor's time
- interruption to work flow.

Few companies attempt to cost their absenteeism, but those that do normally become more concerned with controlling it. The Industrial Society did some work in the early 1970s to try to establish how much, on average, one day's absence cost. The figure that emerged was £70 per day.

3

CAUSES OF ABSENTEEISM

In order for absenteeism to be controlled, it is necessary to understand why it occurs. Although sickness is generally the stated reason, there are often a number of underlying reasons which contribute to the Company's problem. Long-term absences are usually due to genuine illness and should be dealt with in accordance with the procedure outlined in Appendix 1. It is the reasons for persistent short-term absences which have to be examined if major reductions in absenteeism levels are to be attained.

Each organisation will have varying circumstances and it could be a combination of reasons which are causing individuals to take time off. However, these tend to fall into three main categories:

- the company
- the individual
- the environment.

The company

Reasons for absenteeism which are related with the company are usually a result of dissatisfaction with the job or with management. Job related reasons include:

- an employee finding the job boring or repetitive
- poor organisation and inefficient systems
- lack of equipment.

Dissatisfaction with management can be as a result of it:

- being perceived as unfair

- being too autocratic
- being perceived as incompetent
- not treating employees as individuals
- being unable to make decisions
- being too aggressive
- being afraid of confrontation.

The individual

Reasons related with the individual can include:

- personality clashes with managers, supervisors or colleagues
- being incapable of doing the job
- being over-qualified for the job and therefore finding it boring or frustrating
- being unable to cope with the pressure
- being lazy or workshy.

The work environment

A problem arises in this area when absenteeism becomes part of the culture of the organisation. For example, an employee's contract of employment states that they are entitled to six week's full pay for sickness per annum and employees take this to mean that they can take this time off as a right, regardless of whether they are genuinely ill.

Variations

These factors influence absenteeism to varying degrees, depending on the individual organisation and the personalities of those involved. However, research has shown that, atlhough the root causes of absenteeism are probably the same, the problem is more serious in certain sections of the workforce. The Industrial Society survey of 1987 found the following differences.

Regional differences

There is still something of a north–south divide in absence rates. However, the southeast has an absence rate higher than the mean and the northwest's rate is below the mean. The southwest has the lowest absence rate (2.38%). The midlands (6.40%), northeast (5.76%), Scotland (5.44%), and the southeast (5.43%) are above the mean .The northwest (4.60%), eastern region (3.91%), Wales (3.89%), and London (3.31%) are below the mean.

Industry differences

The mean absence rate was lowest in the financial services sector (2.52%) and highest in the transportation/communication industry (8.97%). The other sectors which have low absence rates are construction (2.71%), agriculture/forestry (2.93%), distribution (3.91%), and other services (3.23%). Extraction/chemicals (4.17%), and energy/water (4.29%), are nearer to the average rate. Higher absence rates are found in 'other manufacturing' (6.03%), and engineering (6.50%).

The survey also found that the larger the organisation or the site, the higher the absence rate. The average rate with sites with 1–99 employees is 2.40%. The rate increases to 5.06% at sites with over 1000 employees.

Management, staff and manual differences

In all types of absence—medically certified, self-certified, and uncertificated—manual workers are absent almost twice as much as staff, who themselves are absent almost twice as much as management. Supervisory absence fits almost exactly half-way between staff and management absence. Amongst manual workers, absence is greatest on Mondays.

Differences between males and females

Male staff have less medically certificated absence than females. 56% of female respondents in the survey had an average medically certificated absence at 9 or less days per year. The corresponding figure for males is 70.2%.

There was also a difference in self-certificated absence. The female employees of 25.9% of the respondents were absent more than 7 days, while the male employees of only 17.1% of the respondents were absent.

Full-timers and part-timers

In both the medically certificated and self-certificated categories, there was less absence amongst part-timers than full-timers.

4

ROLES AND FUNCTIONS
IN CONTROLLING
ABSENTEEISM

In order for absenteeism to be controlled effectively, it needs to be clearly identified who has the responsibility for managing it.

One of the factors which influence an individual's decision to stay away from work is whether or not their absence will be questioned or even noticed. Direct control therefore needs to come from someone close to the employee, ideally their line manager or supervisor. The personnel department has the responsibility for ensuring that the standards of absence control required by the organisation are maintained and that the agreed procedures are implemented consistently throughout the company.

The personnel function

As a support service, the personnel department should provide line management with information to enable them to deal effectively with absenteeism. This should include:

- regularly monitoring overall absence rates to enable managers to make comparisons between their and other departments
- analysis of the causes.

Personnel departments also have a role in providing specialist advice and counselling to line managers. This can include:

- dealing with specific individuals
- looking at working practices (e.g. flexible working patterns, attendance bonuses).
- interpreting trade union agreements that control absence (e.g. possible disciplinary action if over a certain percentage)
- providing training in absence control.

The line function

As has been stated, the direct responsibility for controlling absenteeism lies with the line manager or supervisor. An employee needs to know that management are aware of absence records and that disciplinary action is taken when they are unacceptable. Managers should keep records whch enable them to monitor their absenteeism and to identify any trends (e.g. higher than average absences on a Monday).

The role of the trade unions

Where there are trade unions, they should be involved in the drawing up of any procedure for dealing with absenteeism, in order to ensure their commitment. Generally, trade unions are very supportive in this area, recognising the disruption that persistent absenteeism causes to its members.

5

THE CONTRACTUAL FRAMEWORK AND ACAS GUIDELINES

Whenever a person is employed under a contract of employment, then the employer undertakes to provide work and a salary, and the employee undertakes to make themselves available for work. If an employee becomes incapacitated (temporarily or on a longer-term basis) then, in effect, there is a failure to meet these obligations. Consequently, there is a potential breach of contract. However, it is implied that the employee will be away from time to time, but once the incapacity is such that they are unable to fulfil the terms of the contract, then the employer is in a position where they are able to dismiss.

Under the legislation concerning dismissal, one of the fair reasons specified is on the grounds of capability. This can mean qualifications and mental capacity, but also includes situations where the ill-health of an employee is the reason for dismissal. There are two types of ill-health to consider:

1 long term chronically sick employees
2 persistent short-term absences.

Long-term sickness

Long-term ill-health can be a fair reason for dismissal under the heading of capability, provided a proper procedure has been followed. This procedure cannot be a series of warnings as per the disciplinary procedure, as obviously warnings are inappropriate. However, two important cases have given guidelines on how to handle this problem. They are *Spencer* v. *Paragon Wallpapers* (1976) and *East Lindsey District Council* v. *Daubney* (1977).

Spencer v. Paragon Wallpapers (1976) IRLR 373

Mr Spencer had been suffering from a bad back for two months when the Company, who needed everyone at work, approached his doctor to see when he would be fit to return to work. The doctor indicated that it would not be for another four to six weeks. In view of this and the fact that the Company had operational needs, Paragon decided to dismiss Mr Spencer. This dismissal was found to be fair because, in these particular circumstances, the employer could not be expected to wait any longer.

The implications here are, that if you have an employee doing an exclusive job, then there will be a fairly immediate effect on your productivity if they are absent. You therefore have a greater capacity to dismiss than if they are one of many.

East Lindsey District Council v. Daubney (1977) IRLR 181

Mr Daubney was a surveyor and on 29 April 1975 he suffered a mild stroke and remained certificated sick until 30 September 1975. In July 1975, the Personnel Director asked the District Community Physician to indicate whether he felt that Mr Daubney's health was such that he should be retired on grounds of permanent ill-health.

After an examination, it was reported that he should be retired and so Mr Daubney was dismissed. At no point was Mr Daubney consulted and, although efforts had been made to seek medical advice, both the Industrial Tribunal and the Employment Appeals Tribunal (EAT) felt that this was only part of the story.

They felt that discussions and consultations should have taken place, as these will often bring to light facts and circumstances of which the employer was unaware and which will throw new light on the problem. It may also be possible that the employee wishes to seek medical advice on his own account which, brought to the attention of the employer's medical advisers, will cause them to change their opinions.

The dismissal was therefore found to be unfair.

A procedure for dealing with long-term absence through ill-health which takes these findings into account and follows the guidelines given in the ACAS advisory handbook, is given in Appendix 1.

Short-term persistent absences

This type of absenteeism is usually as disruptive as it is unpredictable. As a result, the courts have taken a different view of this type of absence and tend to consider it as a mischievious abuse of generous sick pay schemes, and therefore, a matter of conduct.

There are, again, two leading cases that set out the procedure to follow if a company is considering dismissal on these grounds. They are *International Sports Company Limited* v. *Thompson*, and *Rolls Royce Limited* v. *Walpole.*

International Sports Company v. Thompson (1980) IRLR 340

Mrs Thompson's doctor was given the task of certifying her absences which averaged 25% (against the acceptable level of 8% agreed with the union) and came up with 'dizzy spells, anxiety and nerves, bronchitis, virus infection, cystitis, dyspepsia and flatulence'. Over a period of nine months, she received a string of warnings but her level of absenteeism remained at 22%. The Company doctor was consulted but he realistically expressed the view that no useful purpose would be served by his seeing Mrs Thompson because he could see no common link between the illnesses and there was nothing that could be subsequently verified.

The Industrial Tribunal found the dismissal unfair. The Company appealed to the EAT who reversed the decision. Provided a fair review of the absences takes place and the appropriate warnings are given, an employer is justified in dismissing if absences persist.

Rolls Royce v. *Walpole* (1980) IRLR 340

Mr Walpole was sufficiently young and fit to play rugby regularly and yet, during his last three years of employment, his rate of absence was 44, 35 and 44% respectively. On 23 September 1977, he injured his hand at rugby, causing further absence. He saw his manager on 21 October, who said that if Mr Walpole's doctor agreed, he should return to lighter duties. Before seeing his doctor, Mr Walpole played rugby again and injured his shoulder, extending his absence still more. He was dismissed.

The EAT found the dismissal fair and they coined a phrase which is used in virtually every unfair dismissal case: that it was 'within the range of reasonable responses', to dismiss.

It can be seen from these two cases that persistent absenteeism is considered much more as a disciplinary matter which has more to do with conduct than with capability. Again, the ACAS advisory handbook lays down the procedure to follow and guidelines are given in Appendix 2.

6

CONTROLLING ABSENCE

In order to develop effective policies and procedures for controlling absenteeism, there are a number of areas which need to be considered. A judgement can then be made as to whether they are appropriate for inclusion into the organisation's overall strategy. These include:

- questioning the employee on their return to work
- counselling
- offering attendance bonuses
- reorganising working time
- the procedure for first reporting absence
- harmonisation of sick pay schemes
- use of the disciplinary procedure
- publication of absence statistics
- visiting the absentee.

Questioning the employee on return to work

This should be a key step in any absence control procedure. The fact that the interview takes place shows the employee that the company is concerned with the Individual and that their absence has been noted. This should discourage those that were not genuinely sick from taking time off in the future.

This interview is also an opportunity for the manager or supervisor to discover any underlying reasons for the absence. Care must, however, be taken that these interviews do not become a formality and their effectiveness needs to be monitored regularly.

In a large organisation with a medical department, it may

be appropriate for the employee to be seen by the staff sister. The advantage of this is to give the employee a chance to provide additional information that they were unable or unwilling to give to their manager or supervisor. This is particularly relevant when it is the management that is at the root of the problem.

This procedure should not, however, take away the responsibility for absence from line management. It should be viewed as an additional resource in the management of absence.

Counselling

If an employee has a problem, whether at home or at work, they are more likely to take time off. If the company is able to offer counselling or advice through an employee assistance programme, they may be able to help resolve the situation.

As companies realise the effect that absenteeism has on their profitability, they are beginning to offer additional services to their staff. In some organisations this includes things like marriage guidance and alcohol abuse advice.

Attendance bonuses

Some companies take the view that attendance bonuses are unnecessary, as employees should not be paid twice for coming to work. Others see such payments as an effective way of maximising production or giving a high profile to the subject.

Attendance bonuses do not have to be paid in cash. Other incentives can be offered, such as additional days of holiday. The disadvantages of paying employees these bonuses are that:

● they can be a reflection of weak management
● they can penalise the genuinely sick
● they encourage those who are genuinely sick to report to work

16

- the novelty tends to wear off, with subsequent claims to have the bonus consolidated into basic rates.

However, successful bonus schemes do exist and there are alternative ways of applying the principle. For example, instead of paying an attendance bonus, other rewards such as productivity bonus or profit share could be withheld from employees with poor attendance records.

Re-organising working time

Introduction of flexible working hours can help to avoid casual absences. Many companies cited in IDS Study No. 301 (entitled *Flexible working hours*) reported that this was a major advantage. It enabled employees to have the time to go to the dentist, or to take time off to meet a relative from the station or airport, or it encouraged an employee who has overslept to come to work.

Company procedure for first reporting absence

The procedure should make it clear who they should notify that they will not be attending work and by when. Research has shown that if this is the employee's line manager or supervisor, they are less likely to feign illness than if they can get away with leaving a message with the switchboard or a colleague. If this is established as part of an agreed procedure, non-compliance can then render the employee liable to disciplinary action.

Harmonisation of sick pay schemes

The quality of sick pay schemes within organisations undoubtedly affects absence rates. Some companies feel that the introduction of harmonised schemes will lead to higher rates of absence amongst manual workers as they take advantage of the improved entitlements. Introduction of such schemes has therefore been accompanied by tighter absenteeism controls and, where possible, involved the unions.

However, the answer to the control of absenteeism is more likely to lie in finding out the underlying reasons and motivating the staff than in examining sick pay schemes.

Disciplinary procedure

The disciplinary procedure can be invoked when dealing with short-term persistent absenteeism. However, this should be done in accordance with the guidelines given in Appendix 2.

Some companies have devised formal definitions of unacceptable absence that act as trigger points for taking action. These are useful for two reasons:

● they guide supervisors and line managers as to when warnings should be issued
● application of the disciplinary procedure is consistent.

Publishing absence statistics

The advantage of publishing absence statistics is that it illustrates to employees that absence is taken seriously. The aim is to impress upon employees that their attendance affects the companies productivity and profitability.

Absence statistics can be presented in graph form and pinned to the wall in departments or issued at departmental or briefing group meetings. The key to success is to present the information in a way that is meaningful to the target audience.

Visiting the absentee

Several studies have shown that visits to the employee at home can have a marked effect. The way in which the visit is done, however, is important, as the impression can easily be given that the company is spying, giving rise to resentment of the system. Any policy on sick visiting must, therefore, be applied consistently and include clear guidelines on whose responsibility it is to carry out the visit.

Although visits are usually used with the long-term sick, the effect has been shown to be more valuable if shorter absences are included in the programme.

7

ABSENCE RECORDS

Accurate monitoring and recording of absence is essential to any policy of absence control. Although the actual method of recording will vary depending on the individual requirements of the organisation, the basic purposes of keeping records should be the same:

● to provide information from which to assess whether a problem exists
● to provide information from which analysis can be made of the patterns and types of absenteeism
● to ensure that action can be taken promptly when an individual has a poor record and that any procedure is applied consistently throughout the organisation.

The information required to collate absenteeism statistics can come from a number of sources, including:

● self-certification forms
● absence record cards
● medical notes and records
● statutory sick pay returns
● clock cards
● computerised records.

The 1987 Industrial Society survey found that the most common methods used for discovering absence problems were absence record cards and self-certification forms, medical forms and statutory sick pay. Less popular were computers and time checks.

However, detailed statistics cannot be produced manually without many hours of work. Companies should be looking at ways of computerising their records to enable them to produce meaningful information on absenteeism patterns. This will help to identify and then deal with problems.

The information should:

- give overall absence levels for the organisation
- categorise the reasons, i.e. sickness, maternity, industrial action
- give comparisons of absence levels between departments
- give statistics over a rolling 12 month period to identify whether absence levels are deteriorating or improving and the extent of annual, seasonal and weekly trends.

The responsibility for maintaining absence records will depend on the organisation and needs of the company. Line managers should have responsibility for controlling absenteeism within their own departments and should therefore keep records. However, if the system is computerised it might be more appropriate for the records to be compiled centrally on the basis of information received from each department. Even in this case, line managers can still keep their own records of individuals' attendance within their department.

8

POSITIVE ACTION
TO REDUCE ABSENTEEISM

Accountability

- Define who is responsible for monitoring absence.
- Ensure that line managers understand that they are responsible for controlling absence in their teams.

Interviews

- Ensure that line managers interview their employees on their return to work to determine the reasons for their absence.

Records

- Ensure that line managers keep adequate and meaningful records.
- Ensure that patterns of absence are looked at monthly and annually.

Communication

- Ensure that employees are aware that management are concerned with absence.
- Where appropriate, involve the trade union in order to build commitment to dealing with the problem.

Sanctions

- Ensure that employees understand the consequences of abusing the system.
- Be prepared to take the disciplinary route when dealing with short-term persistent absence.

APPENDICES

APPENDIX I

LONG-TERM ABSENCE THROUGH ILL-HEALTH—PROCEDURES

1 The employee should be contacted periodically and, in turn, should maintain regular contact with the employer.

2 The employee should be kept fully informed if employment is at risk.

3 The employee's GP should be asked when a return to work is expected and of what type of work the employee will be capable.

4 On the basis of the GP's report, the employer should consider whether alternative work is available.

5 The employer is not expected to create a special job for the employee concerned, nor be a medical expert, but to take action on the basis of the medical evidence.

6 Where there is reasonable doubt about the nature of the illness or injury, the employee should be asked to agree to be examined by a doctor appointed by the company.

7 Where an employee refuses to co-operate in providing medical evidence or to undergo an independent medical examination, the employee should be told in writing that a decision will be taken on the basis of the information available and that it could result in dismissal.

8 Where an employee is allergic to a product used in the workplace, the employer should consider remedial action or a transfer to alternative work.

9 Where the employee's job can no longer be kept open and no suitable alternative work is available, the employee should be informed of the likelihood of dismissal.

10 Where the dismissal action is taken, the employee should be given the period of notice to which they are entitled and informed of any right of appeal.

See ACAS Advisory Booklet No. 5: *Absence* (1985).

APPENDIX II

PERSISTENT SHORT-TERM ABSENCE— PROCEDURES

1 Absences should be investigated promptly and the employee asked to give an explanation.

2 Where there is no medical advice to support frequent self-certificated absences, the employee should be asked to consult a doctor to establish whether medical treatment is necessary and whether the underlying reason for absence is work related.

3 If, after investigation, it appears that there were no good reasons for the absences, the matter should be dealt with under the disciplinary procedure.

4 Where absences arise from temporary domestic problems, the employer, in deciding appropriate action, should consider whether an improvement in attendance is likely.

5 In all cases, the employee should be told what improvement is required and warned of the likely consequences if this does not happen.

6 If there is no improvement, the employee's age, length of service, performance, the likelihood of a change in attendance, the availability of suitable alternative work and the effect of past and future absences on the business, should all be taken into account when deciding on appropriate action.

7 It is essential that persistent absence is dealt with promptly, firmly, and consistently, in order to show both the employee concerned and other employees, that absence is regarded as a serious matter and may result in dismissal. An examination of records may identify those employees who are regularly absent and may show an absence pattern. In such cases, employers should make sufficient enquiries to determine whether the absence is because of genuine illness or for other reasons.

See ACAS Advisory Booklet No. 5: *Absence* (1985).